The Way to the River

The Way to the River

Poems by

Shutta Crum

Cover design by Shay Culligan
Front Cover photo by Jakob Owens on Unsplash
Back Cover photo by Clint Mccoy on Unsplash

ISBN: 978-1-63980-088-9

Kelsay Books
502 South 1040 East, A-119
American Fork, Utah 84003
Kelsaybooks.com

. . . with love for Fred W.
SC

Acknowledgments

My gratitude goes out to the AAR2 which has consistently published my poems since the 1970s! Thank you, my friends. Another big thank you goes to Betsy Baier for her eagle eyes in proofreading everything. And to all the hard-working folks at poetry/literary journals who strive to make sure creative work can be shared, kudos! Poets would be lost without you. And I would, certainly, be lost without the support of my family and my poetry loving friends. Finally, this comes with a special thanks to the publishers who have previously published several of these poems.

Beyond Words: "How to Properly Read a Paper Map."

3rd Wednesday: "Reading Brodsky (in English) While Stirring Soup."

Redshift: "On the Beach."

Southern Poetry Review: "The Canoeist."

Passenger: "Lavender Doe."

Main Street Rag: "Everything is Far."

AAR2: "Paleontology in Such a Land," and "Always there are Mothers."

The Collection (Footprints): "After You."

Typehouse Literary: "We Meet for Coffee at a Crowded Café," "Baptized at the Creek," and "The Pittance."

Plainsongs: "All That is Left."

Contents

Water in the Lungs

Where the Dark Wild Closes In

Everything is Far

Why Poetry

Why Poetry

Poems are mini stories, fleeting images, quick gestures of recognition and a lilt of music for the soul. A volume of poetry is a colorful collage of those stories, images, gestures, and musical tones from a life.

When you look at a collage you notice parts merge into other parts, or twist away in denial, or build upon one another. You might recognize a corner here, or an applied piece there. But in experiencing the overall effect you begin to understand the dance of all the parts. The same applies to poetry. How do the poems in a book work together? Does the volume move effortlessly from one moment, or poem, to the next? Or is it intentionally rough going? Are there places where you must stop to close your eyes, to catch a breath, or to gaze out quietly? Do any dark purposeful pitfalls later rise into glorious high views of an examined life? Were you meant to be fearful at one poem, disgusted at another, and enamored at others?

However the whole is sensed, I hope you enter these poems savoring a moment of recognition, smelling a day from your childhood, or hearing a voice you had almost forgotten. But first, go to the kitchen and get a slice of pie.

Poetry should be experienced with pie.

Poetry and pie—forever!
Shutta

Aboutness

Some words have smooth cheeks,
like *café au lait*
which a thumb has lovingly stroked.

Like *peach,* that ease of voluptuous
dawn slipping out of its bath robe.

Some words are too brittle, anorexic.
For example: *black.*
For example: *white.*

When we come to each other,
let us come with words
whose cheeks invite us to kiss them,
with big-bodied words that awe us,

and with words that hold
a soft and generous aboutness
in this space between us.

How Poetry Reframes the Moment

Take, for example,
the gravel you kicked up on the farm lane.
With a twist of memory,
it becomes eroding words between brothers—
the field between them unplowed.

Or catch the sound of a tree
as it groans against another, crescendo-ing
into the misfiring of your grandfather's tractor.
The old International Harvester
grinding off into the bluster of years.

Or reframe the way water
undermines the banks of the creek bed.
Now, it's the arthritis eating at the dust-colored dog—
known only as *Boy*—
who always cranked himself up to greet you at the gate.

Or observe how a day takes its time devolving into night.
Isn't that the same as the blackening of the wax seals
on your grandmother's canned green beans?
Tireless Mason Jar sentinels.

And that *thump-crack!* of a log-splitter echoing
repeatedly from your uncle's farm next door? Reframe that,
and it's your grandmother's scarred hands plucking
and slapping at the wrinkles in the checkered tablecloth
when they told her of your grandfather's last worship—
fallen, spread-eagled, upon the stubbled earth he'd loved.

Now, look out toward the hedgerow in the distance.
Know that it scratches a ragged line in the dirt.
Fold it inward and remember the crumpled letter
shoved to the back of a drawer in your grandparents' room,

and the single silk stocking you found in a heart shaped box—
its dark seam woven of regret.

Then stand still amid the persistence of fireflies
and the sheer doggedness of that thin wind from the creek.
For the poet, that's become the stubborn run of seasons
wearying the abandoned International to rust,
and the silence just after your grandmother muttered,
"Who's going to harvest the melons?"

Of Maps and Their Roads

The Highway of the Three Graces

Slump-shouldered—still,
it was the kind of road
that furthered dreams.

I sealed a toe-print into the warm tar of it
when I was young and sure of heart,
trusting it would know when I was ready.

Years later,
the road muscled into memory
unfolding like a lover from sleep.

Now, after many miles, I've earned a milk crate
from the three graces.
I sit upon it with my sign: *Go. Witness. Speak.*

I watch for pilgrims—
the highway patched, but still fetching.

How to Properly Read a Paper Map

Put away your electronics.
Find a map your father used on road trips—
the one that billowed in the front seat,
Mom's finger racing across it.

Unfold the map and smooth it flat
in the middle of the floor.
Walk around it, biting into a sandwich.
Stare down at the names of cities:
Moab, Grayling, Micanopy, Bug Spit.
Imagine the society of town namers.

Wonder if fog floats above Mystic Seaport,
if distance is deceptive in the Badlands,
if desert winds blow hot from Joshua Tree,
if the fertile hollers of Tomahawk
and Rockcastle exhale memories—
rich and smelling of rivers.

Pour yourself a glass of milk.
Drink it, while studying the countryside
caught in the creases. Notice how one fold
rises like an offering. Watch for a road
that reaches out to touch your foot.
Maybe just a thin thread—an idea of a road.

It's cold. Put on pajamas and socks.
Circle the map again, listening
to the way it shifts and settles.
Go into the kitchen. Stare into space a moment.
Search for a cookie.

In the morning, find that thread of road
tangled in the fringe of your rug.
Take it to the window. Lift it close.
See how it twists, catching the light?

When you go, dress warmly.
Drive slowly.
Wave often.

Farnsworth Road

My childhood street feels foreign—
ill-fitting against the soles of my feet.
I find a stone along the ditch.
Pocket it for luck, for protection,
for absolution of whatever youthful crimes
I committed.

There was inattention
to other lives—to you—
that customary blinkering of youth.
I did not see you living a different life.

How can that be?
You roamed backyards with me—
tousle-haired, sun-burnished.

Summers we spent on beaches—
heavy with the smell
of lake water, lotion, wet towels.
And in the distance, always,
the laughter of parents.

Winters were spent in tight boots,
and second-hand coats, chins and noses
muffled in wool scarves wet from our breathing.
Me, holding your mittened hand.

There were years in the same school
with those same boots lining the hallway.
The damp as pervasive as the smell
of bologna sandwiches, wet socks, chalk.
Then the walk home along the ditch.
I threw a rock. Someone bled. You?

Now, the road home is subversive.
It folds in upon itself fashioning a windowscape.
And you there—I see you now, looking out at me.
Your beauty quickens with my fear of losing it.
I rub my thumb along the smoothness
of the stone in my pocket.

Coming into Maggie Valley

Early—
our car downshifting as we rise.
Around us, mountain tops arrayed
in turbans of fog.

Inhaling clouds,
we're closer to heaven here.
When we crest the ridgeline,
the fog tatters.

Coming down into the valley,
we float through the diaphanous breath
of these mountains,
redolent of rivers and of an elder Earth—
an ancestry I know well.

Soon, we'll stop for gas.
We'll stretch our legs on the cracked concrete
of a Sunoco station.
I'll stare up at the stooped backs of these mountains
and remember whose daughter I am.

In a Softer Time

life
wore its edges rounded
summer-blurred and perfumed
by rising bread, mown grass, lilacs

fathers
wore bowling shirts on weekends
other days, they carried black lunch pails
to work—packed with sandwiches
laughed when you needed rescuing from trees
lavished kisses on banged-up knees

mothers
wore shirt-waisted dresses
but helped you build forts
in the field next door
then, laughing, washed you in the tub
with brothers and sisters

sidewalks
wore boutonnières of marigolds
on their sculpted lapels
and across backyards
clothes hung wet-slapping from lines
until sheets, wind-stiffened
smelled like clouds

we
wore our aliveness like shields
as we ventured to the green tousled ends
of the world—warriors all
or so it seemed

Someone to Ride Shotgun

Hitchhiker

He was thumbing it
by the Kroger's parking lot
with a sign that read:
skin—summer—taste—flicker.

So, I picked him up
in a time of silent horizons.
For a long while we rode together
barely speaking.
We were shy with each other.

When a whiff of patchouli
from younger days made us smile,
I longed for my muse
to launch into rhythmic conversation.

But he insisted on stopping
to walk mutely along ditches to a flicker
of gold or lavender flowering in
the crumbling tarmac. Always,
we agreed it was worth the stop.

And once, during a long and desolate stretch,
I laid my hand nakedly upon his leg.
He let it rest there, in the space between us—
his skin becoming a membrane of summer music,
his tongue tasting like the last golden
flicker of childhood.

We Meet for Coffee at a Crowded Café

We bend across the table—two huddled penitents.
Between us coffee, scones, and the dance of your hands
touching the salt and pepper, picking up and replacing
the menu in its metal cage, sweeping specters of crumbs
to the floor—as though dictated
by some mad ricketed choreographer.

I whisper, "Stop." And press your palms into each other
in the warm cradle of my own. "Breathe. Look at me."
I know, already, of the bruised jewels you wear
always hidden under cuffs—of the contract made real
with the pressing of his seal upon you.

It is always the subtle injustices one notices first.
Perhaps it was the precision of each of his syllables—
the authorial *we* angled into eddies of conversation—
as though your life was subtext. His: *We are fine.*

Perhaps it was the flat of his hand at the rare party,
riding low on your back and steering you swiftly by
for the occasional glimpse from friends.
But never through the crowds to this café.

Never here, where you have finally made your way
like some dazed animal come forward
to finger iron bars for the first time.

Shh-h-h. Drag your eyes from the crowd behind me.
Bow with me across this table. Over these simple coffees
we will plan a mutiny.

Reading Brodsky (in English) While Stirring Soup

—for Joseph Brodsky

At almost 600 pages
it's hard to hold the heavy volume
and stir the soup—root vegetables and beans.
15 varieties it says on the package.
Now, one nation of bean.

Joseph's poems (I feel I can call him that),
are visual and intimate.
I stop often to stare out the window
past the palms to Russian winters
with their wool-clad women scissoring
homeward on horizons.
I stir only when recalled
by the hubbub of the beans.
The soup, on its last hour,
is mushroomy, thick, fragrant of salt,
of earthiness—hugging the pot.
I'm fearful of its burning,

like Joseph bursting
from the café in Yalta his heart afire.
Joseph, hurtling into that unrelenting future,
into that blustering cold
which will rattle the shafts of horses
and fill the wind-bucketed shawls of women.

His poems are hearty.
Thickened by root and want,
they've simmered in dimly lit rooms
that one is always entering or leaving.

Tonight, I've invited him to sit at my table
where there is beer, brown bread, and this soup
I've mothered all day.

Navigation

The couch rises a few inches, drifts sleepily past.
The book you laid on the coffee table lifts—the coffee table too.
All the accoutrements of a marriage float—we're in no danger.
They bob with ease and humble elegance—
my shoes, the television set, pictures of the children, our bedding.
And sparkling upward, the lost earring I'd fretted over.
I open my hand and it wafts onto my palm.

I turn and you are here, beside me, navigating this life.
Mid-current we gaze toward an oil slick. It does not break apart,
sink, or dissolve. It has found some anchorage amid our days—
work, appointments, plans, your cancer, my fears.

This morning, we do not mention the dark stain awash with us
as the couch nudges the back of my leg for attention,
as you hold out your cup. As coffee—sweetened—
floats effortlessly to my lips.

Entwined

A lightness of the heart wakens me.
And I lie, hand on chest, lingering
over each knotted love on the cord of my life.

It is a wondrous thing
to have a life woven of such strong silk—
each turning of the cord so precise,
beloved histories are reclaimed.
Each twist known so intimately,
voices and scents fill me.
Each love there when I need to hold on.
There, when I do not know I need to hold on.

I touch these familiar knots
on my counting cord with reverence.
There is no place, no time,
in which I am: one.
All my loves are entwined.

You are here, too.

Wading Out

At the River

when I can
I let the impatient wind push me
into canyons intimate with water
there I cast for half-notions
or jig for a whispered voice

if the sun
hints at a shadow beneath the surface
I plunge my hands downstream of it
sometimes I pull up a discarded bicycle tire
or a rainbow to gut
sometimes it's a prize to stretch out in the sun

then, I'll anchor
one corner of it with a rock
knowing all acts are gestures of recognition
an upwelling of the gilled breath
I did my many trout lives ago
of this human breathing I do now
millennia later

eddies and riffles
backflow into something resembling a life
so why not roll up pant-legs
and wade out along the shoal
fingers outstretched for the fat belly of a catch

to pull it out,
pin it down with a rock
study its scale, its drift, its hunger to spawn

The River When It Rains

"No osprey today," you say,
just as the rain moves in
swaddling the sky in wool.
Rainwater pelts river water.
What is beyond is gone.
The distant shore's a ghost.
In rain, the world shrinks.
You open an umbrella
and put an arm around me.
Our universe is smaller, now,
but infinitely vast.

Baptized at the Creek

All us kids stood—wide-eyed. Cousin Billy
stuck his thumb in his mouth, as they laid Aunt Gertie backward
under the brown waters of the creek.

Right then and there, sacredness came floating 'round us.
The holler got so warm and holy I could hardly breathe.
I reached out and squeezed Sissy's hand.

Aunts and uncles, standing witness, shouted *Hallelujah!*
and raised their arms to heaven. Billy peed on a tree.
We giggled. Uncle Winn snagged him with his arm.
Grandpa prayed.
                    Praise the Lord!

When they helped Aunt Gertie up the bank of the creek
her clothes clung sopping over her rounder parts,
the way honey clings to a biscuit. I tried not to look.

We ate corn bread, fried chicken, green beans and ham hocks,
homemade rolls, canned peaches, and Grandma's pies.
Billy wiggled, corralled between Uncle Winn and Grandpa.

Cousin Louann played the guitar. Her boyfriend, the harmonica.
Sissy swung Billy round and round. Aunt Dixie and Uncle Walter
Lee sang—
their mournful voices rising and then swooping deep, flowing into
us.
                    Praise the Lord!

Later, in the cool dew-fall hour, we went back to the creek.
We chased fireflies and threw stones into the water. Too dark to see
the ripples widen. But we knew they lapped ashore—washing
away our sins.

Moab

Water scores rock.
It takes millennia. Yet,
intention never wavers.
I kneel, and blow the dust away
from the boulder we've pulled
ourselves upon.
My fingers find traceries—
the ancient signature of water.

The heat-hazy morning quavers,
holding its blue-gray breath.
We wipe sweat from our faces
and do not hurry—
mindful of the engraver's task,
and a teardrop's track.

On the Beach

Boys in sea-soaked swim trunks
skim rocks across the waves. A few skip,
then sink resolutely after
having spent centuries rolling in the surf,
smoothing edges, destroying evidence
of ancient algae, reptile tread, soot-filled skies.

The stones had come to rest on this beach.
Here, where summer-glistened boys
bend over them, studiously selecting,
turning each over and over in the ancestral
salt that wells up from the palms of their hands.

Then drooping trunks are pulled up,
legs are braced and eyes squeezed
to squint across the unknown deep.
It's a small betrayal—
played out with a simple side-arm fling.

Above the Strandline

—after Rachel Carson

If you want me,
I'm making my way up from the bladder wrack
or burrowing in beach sand—
cognizant that if one's anchored
for long above the tide line
the liquescent life begins to lose its hold.

The assault of tides—the battering,
the stretching, has made me rounder,
more seasoned against the storm surge
and the travail of the rockweed.

I know some who carry close
saltwater in their limpid shells,
for our kind have not long been breathers of air.
We are wary of that thin illusion of connection
and are prone to the benediction of the salt.

For me, a tidal pool above the strandline
is an estrangement to which I go willingly—
one I might slip my foot into.

Water in the Lungs

The Pittance

His son was born in the middle of a thunderstorm,
on the seat of his '41 Mercury. The river so high
it spat whole trees up from its churning gut.
No way to get to the hospital.

He stood in the rain, waiting for someone—
anyone—to tell him what he already knew.
She was dead. *What a waste of a good woman.*
And now, him with a baby he'd not wanted.

The Big Sandy chomped at his feet, chewing its way
up to the road. He thought about driving the Merc in.
Wondered what it'd feel like—swallowing
that muddy water—that dirt he dug his hands into every day.
Wondered if she'd already be there when he passed from this life—
waiting—hangdog look and all.

He pulled at his wet hair, swiped the water from the window,
and stared in at his dead woman and at that pittance of a thing
wrapped in her old sweater—its tiny face red with rage.

Years Later, Water Lilies

against the sluggish current
lily pads rise, settle
a tendril lifts—something noses below

someone lost? I wondered
as a young voice called to me
years ago—someone lost?
and still, I stand and stare at black water
wondering who it is that's lost

trying to recall the cries
nightly culled from a mother
the heavy pacing of a father
the groaning through months, years
spent on the tugging of a thing so deep
impossible to root out

someone lost?
who's asking? I ask

the late season blossoms are gone
wilted? torn? never plucked—
you could tip a boat over
trying to wrench one free
but the floating leaves remain, placid
in this bright, formidable light
someone lost?

a push through reeds and arrowroot
a shock of cold water
licking the tops of bare feet
at the river, again, there's a reckoning
for what was left unanswered

there—just there—something
a stealthy movement
a primitive fear nosing in the mud
someone lost at the root?

I point it out to you
it was you that asked, wasn't it?

Lavender Doe

—cold case closed, Kilgore, TX

Twelve years ago, the townsfolk
gave her what they could—
a sweet name and a gravestone.
No simple *Jane Doe.*

Lavender Doe,
for the very little that remained—
a bit of lavender shirt,
perfect teeth and $40 in her jeans.

I like to think that her grave
lies far from oil derricks.
That it overlooks a river
or a pasture full of cows.
That she rests in the rustling music
from cottonwood trees.

I like to think that some in town
bring flowers. And those perfect teeth
want to smile.
I like to think that someone misses her.

Assaulted, murdered, partially burned—
twelve years she lay unclaimed
until he struck again.

At last, her name returned: Dana.
Dana Lynn Dodd, age 21.
Lavender shirt. Perfect teeth.
A sister who misses her.

And the $40?
"Because," her killer said,
"she earned it."

After You

the pine you slashed, bleeds
I dip a finger into sap—taste

the sweetness hits first, then the tang
knifing up through nasal passages
the bite—sharp
oh yes, you've come this way

I kneel
run a finger over the scar
your shoe made in the mud
a disfigurement recognizable
by the ridging on the right
deeper there—those shoes
laced tight for lashing out

farther on
a young willow, slender branched
but crippled—the bent limb
another sign of your trespass

yes—I'm here, again
trailing you through the scrublands
bandaging the wounded
wondering what door you jimmied
to escape and machete through my memory

Always, there are Mothers

In any battle there are always mothers.
Who will grieve with them—
with the mothers who patiently knit
dark hours into tangled shrouds?

And what of the one in the watery lair?
What of Grendel's mother who thirsts
for Beowulf, for the bee-hunter—bear—
but tastes only the blood of her child?

Who will grieve with her?
She who rocked her beastly boy—
      kept his corpse
      and mourned.
She who pledged revenge on the hero
      of the honeyed veins,
      of the weak eyes,
on the hero who laughed as he dove
      into the murk
      and her tentacled embrace,
on the hero who knew nothing
      of a mother's love
      and a mother's oath.

In any battle there are always mothers.
And there is grief—
that exquisite knot of righteousness,
      shining.
Shining, as mothers crowd pews,
as hands dip into sacred water
baptizing golden bee-boys
—never the sons of the dark one.

Shining, these new babes—radiant Beowulfs.
One day they will be lifted from the frontlines
and laid into the arms of mothers.

In any battle there are always mothers.
Even there, in the dark recess
where one weeps for Grendel.

Where the Dark Wild Closes In

The Canoeist

He travels the river—
raising only a ripple fore and aft.
His paddle perfects silver spirals
upon the surface. The only sound
the plink and plonk of water
as he dips into stillness.

He passes homes,
manicured lawns, boat docks.
He hears children. People wave,
or stare from their deck chairs.
A heron rises from the reeds.

Now, fewer watch his passing.
He will not return.
They know well what is downstream
where the current stalls,
where cattails, water lilies,
spatterdocks encroach, and roots catch.

Of an evening, some will walk
to the water's edge and listen
for the distant plying of his paddle,
or the subtle wash of his passage
across the surface of the night.
They will breathe in the river damp,
knowing he is out there
where the dark wild closes in.

Things Done Wrong

—for Mom (1933-2008)

Forgive me—
when you left, I forgot
to harvest the poems
that had taken root
in the floodplain of your hands.

I forgot to bathe
naked in the river-light
that buoyed your bed.

I forgot to fend off
that pale moon-faced boatman—
nightshade tucked neatly
in his buttonhole—tiller ready.

It is only now,
when I wake and wade into the river,
that I call out to that patient
gentleman . . . *Wait! Wait!*

As though he could see my arms waving.
As though he knew we were old friends.
As though he'd turn his boat about,
and return what was mine.

All That is Left

remorse is a small sad word
uncapitalized, it resides in voices
lost in the dry hollows of bones
and in the dust
when that is all that is left

before the first word
before the first gesture
before the first gasp from the first lung
remorse waited in the dirt

my trail from the womb of the sea
was carved by countless bellies
worn resolutely through centuries of remorse
i followed and did not stop
thinking there must be more ahead—more

and yet, i keep glancing back
to the loveliness of that first nursery
to the buoyancy and taste of salt
to the starlight glinting on waves above me

to the lullabies of my first mother—her seasong
adrift through remorse and the bones of those i've loved
one day she'll sift through the dust of another lost child
when that is all i've come to

Paleontology in Such a Land

—after Loren Eiseley

timeless sandstone
dry waste
and a crack carved

in the shifting light
bone gleams
   sand-filled sockets
   a skull

I, too, am a future fossil
of former lives
  of fern damp
  of croakings
  of mindless nights
    clinging
    to the evolutionary tree

now, lifting bones
into light
  each shard
  a reminder
of what will be
my own broken wilderness

Everything is Far

Everything is Far

—after Rainer Maria Rilke's "Lament"

Like you, my friend . . .
no matter how many times
I walk under the wide sky
I can't walk out of my heart.
This soul I carry is caught tight.
So, I suspect, was yours.
It's a restless confinement, though—
pulling at doors, walking barefoot
beneath trees, crazily imagining
I might follow your gaze
and see that white city
in the light of a star that still blazes.

The cry of a lone nighthawk
wavers above abandoned streets.
Like me, she is flying through endings—
stopped clocks and voices cut short.
If I stretch into the limitless heavens
might I catch a consoling word?
Might I feel the blessings of a dusky sky
and find forgiveness in the ancient light
that has taken millennia to find me here,
aching for you?

Tell me,
is your white city bathed in poem-light,
or in a radiance you've woven
into the battlements of prayer?

In a House by the School
I Consider the Lilies of the Field

I throw down my dish towel and gulp my coffee,
hoping to burn through my thoughts.
We are told to consider the lilies.
How they toil not, and neither do they spin.

Yet, watching from my kitchen window,
I see such small serious faces. The children trudge past
with their backpacks. Cast out, already,
from the Garden. They will toil. Certainly,
some will rise above the fields and blaze like galaxies.
Some will fire and scorch the land only to sputter out.
Some will never ignite—their toil barely acknowledged.

I dump the last of the coffee and grab at the sink
to keep myself from running into the street.
I want to stop this growing away from their first flowering.
I want to pull them to me and hold them, flawless—
for I have so little faith in fragile futures.

What I want to shout is: See?
My hands and my heart are calloused with toil.
Every day I labor in this clay-bound body.
Run into the fields. Toil not. And neither should you spin.
Become, instead, that playful twitch at the corner of God's mouth.

Mausoleums

—after Ruth Rendell, *Dreadful Day of Judgement*

in *the little houses of the dead*
there are no tables or little plates
no one waits to eat

beyond the crypts, over the graveyard wall
lies a field where, in the distance, cows graze
and a farmer walks bent against the angle of the Earth

i am crossing that field
consulting my guidebook, checking my itinerary
no ordinary tourist

i am not lured to memorials by architectural details
not by gargoyles, or angels, or the capitals of columns
supporting little porticos

it is the impermanence of these lives
played out on little stages
with large consequences that enlivens me

it is the whiff of ancient must, a complex fragrance
so particular and cunning—the smell of memories
that makes my heart feel lighter

these lives housed in these little houses
how immense the weight of their individual loves
how tangled their loathings

i will stand here a long time
by the broken urn, by the padlocked portal
by the well-earned weathering

of these little houses of the dead
until night falls and i
no longer need a guidebook

No Mansions for Me

When I arrive in Heaven
I want to float through star-littered fields.
I want to bathe naked in the Euphrates when it was young.

When I arrive
I'd like a welcoming committee of puppies.
And a small orchestra of penguins playing cellos.

On some days in Heaven
I want to stand in the silent chapel of a pine forest in winter.
Or wander, following the smell of the ocean.

On other days
I want to be overpowered by the scent of cicely,
or a meadow that blossoms every night and smells like rain.

What else?
I want to sleep adrift in birdsong, curled under the 49 quilts
made by my mother with her strong hands.

But first
I want my father to sing one of those corny songs
about betting it all on love.

You know the kind.
Where a poor man wins the heart of a local lovely.
But then . . .

Well, maybe not *that* song.
Death's too definite to be sung into being.

Other times, let me taste the sweetest of windswept memories.
Maybe, the night my love and I lay in the bed of the pick-up truck,
high on a mesa, and watched the moon watching us.

Or one of the times he lifted my face to his
while the world lost all its words in all its languages.

Yes, that will do.
That will do nicely when I arrive in Heaven.

About the Author

Shutta Crum is an award-winning poet and children's book writer, as well as an oft-requested speaker and presenter at writing conferences, libraries, and schools. Shutta's poems have appeared in many journals since the 1970s. Numerous poems have been published by the *AAR2* over the years. (The online Ann Arbor Review.) Other poems were published by *ArtAscent, Blue Mountain Review, Typehouse, Stoneboat, the Orchards Poetry Journal, 3rd Wednesday, Nostos, Beyond Words, Southern Poetry Review, Better Than Starbucks, Main Street Rag, Plainsongs.* Forthcoming: *Mom Egg Review.* Her chapbook WHEN YOU GET HERE won a gold Royal Palm Literary Award. She is, also, the author of three novels for young readers and many children's picture books including, THUNDER-BOOMER! (Clarion/HMH) a *Smithsonian Magazine* and an *American Library Association Notable Book* of the year. In 2005 she was invited to read at the White House, and in 2010 toured Japan presenting to students of the Dept. of Defense schools.

Shutta was nominated for a Pushcart Prize in 2020 by Typehouse Literary for her poem "We Meet for Coffee at a Crowded Café." (Included within.)

THE WAY TO THE RIVER is a confluence of Shutta's earlier published poems with several new ones.

Contact Shutta at:

Website ~ shutta.com

Facebook ~ facebook.com/Shuttacrum

Twitter ~ @Shutta

Instagram ~ instagram.com/Shuttacrum

Praise for WHEN YOU GET HERE
by Shutta Crum
(Chapbook, Kelsay Books, 2020)

"Here's everything you want in poetry. Understandable language—check. Interesting, inventive use of words—check. Topics that reference matters of common interest—check. Insights way beyond the usual—check. Don't skim this collection. You'd miss way too much that makes our lives meaningful. Enter and walk "unafraid in this new topography."

Sharon Scholl, Professor emerita of humanities.
Author of *Music and Culture, Death and the Humanities,*
and three chapbooks of poetry.

www.ingramcontent.com/pod-product-compliance
Lightning Source LLC
Chambersburg PA
CBHW031150090426
42738CB00008B/1286